Devotions
for
Your Family

Marjorie Bloom

Devotions
for
Your Family

WORD BOOKS
PUBLISHER
WACO, TEXAS

Devotions for Your Family

ISBN 0-8499-2836-2
Library of Congress catalog card number: 78-59462
Printed in the United States of America

Preface

God has impressed upon me the supreme importance of family Bible study. He has led me to realize that the home is the foundation for learning and has caused me to want my children, above all else, to receive a sound spiritual upbringing. I know of no other way to teach them than to share my faith and belief in God with them and to let them see his love in me.

I want to thank my pastor, the Reverend Jack Green, and my husband, Jim, for their advice, encouragement, and support as I have written this book.

It is my prayer that God will use this book to help many families to find guidance, closeness, and spiritual growth in a time when it is so greatly needed.

Introduction

As we face the continuing disintegration of family life in America, nothing more appropriate could be offered to rebuild the home in all that it means to the life of the people than a worthy series of suggested daily devotions. You will find just such a series in this magnificent book entitled, "Devotions for Your Family—Sharing in a Study of Mark." Each day a pericope of the gospel is selected in continuity, and the passage is placed in a format in which the child, the teenager, and the adult can beautifully share.

It took a great deal of work to prepare such a volume as is presented in this study, but it is eminently, even pre-eminently, worth it. Mrs. Marjorie Bloom has brought honor and glory to our Savior in these passages, and the felicitous results will be seen in the blessing these devotions bring to uncounted thousands of homes.

It is my prayer that God will aboundingly reward every family that places a copy of this book on the table where the members of the group can gather around and read and witness and pray together.

W. A. Criswell
Pastor, First Baptist Church
Dallas, Texas

The Whys and Wherefores of Family Bible Study

Family Bible study? What for? How? When? With our busy schedule?

Today's family members are very busily involved in their own separate tasks. The family has very little time together as a whole. But suppose that you set aside and insist that for at least fifteen minutes of each day your family will open God's Word together. What benefits will you realize?

You will find out how much your children know or don't know about God, his Son, the plan of salvation, and the Bible. What better place to lead a child to Christ than in the home?

You will gain insight into some of the guilts, frustrations, temptations, sorrows, joys, etc. that each family member faces and be able to lead them to an understanding of how God can help them deal with these experiences.

You can give your family the sound moral and ethical teachings that are sometimes difficult to approach in any other way. Often these principles can be instilled before problems arise, thus averting a crisis.

You can help your child to understand that, although you value the teaching and practice of piano, swimming, baseball, intellectual pursuits, and all the other things the family sets aside time for, the learning of God's Word is of utmost importance. Bible knowledge, memorization of Scripture, and a sound prayer life are things your child will carry with him throughout his life. That he learned to do this at home, with his family, will also stay with him throughout his life and will hopefully be carried out in his future family.

"But when can a busy family such as ours possibly find a time to all be together?" you may ask. The problem of time may be the hardest problem you will have to deal with. You must discuss with your family your desire to have a family altar and discuss what suggestions they have for a time that will most easily accommodate everyone. Someone will probably have to compromise. The best time for some is the first thing in the morning, thus setting a pattern for the day. Even if you are not normally an early riser, you may want to try it. For others, the best time is after supper—before dessert! Once you have decided on a time, you should stay with that time in order to form a consistent, regular time that the family can look forward to and count on. If one member of the family cannot always be present, proceed at that time anyway, and let him participate when he is able.

There are some definite dos and don'ts that, in my opinion, should be incorporated in order for this to be an enjoyable, well-received time of worship. Family worship should be a happy time, not an obligation, and your attitude will set the pace. Everyone should be encouraged to participate—from setting Bibles around to picking out applicable materials. The more you involve people, the more wholeheartedly they will participate. If you have some tiny tots, you may want to give them something quiet to look at or do so that they can also be present at this time.

This time should be used to build up and encourage—never to criticize, discipline, or point a finger at any particular individual and thus embarrass or alienate him. A loving, sharing family time should be the prevailing theme. If you have company, encourage them to join you. What a fun way for your children to learn to witness to their friends.

The leader of the worship time should gear the questions to fit his or her own family in both age level and Bible maturity level. For example, sometimes a question will have to be reworded in order for the whole family to understand what is being discussed.

There are many methods to use for a family worship time. Probably Dad will want to lead the family, but if Dad isn't so inclined, then Mom will probably inherit this responsibility. You may want to discuss materials with your family and let them suggest what they would like to include. You may want to use things like music, puppets, skits, stories, or visual aids as part of your study. A varied plan helps keep the interest level high. A good guideline, however, is to keep your worship time simple, relatively brief, and above all, consistent.

How to Use This Book

Devotions for Your Family contains a study of the Book of Mark through inductive questions geared to each age group in the family.

There are three distinct sections to each lesson. First, there is a time of informal family discussion; second, a time of Bible reading and study; and third, a time of prayer.

The discussion time should be a time of sharing and getting to know each other's thoughts. Everyone should be encouraged to participate and each person should be allowed to express his ideas freely without fear of criticism or argument.

The Bible study section should be conducted with the idea that each person will understand all he can about what God has to say in that day's portion of Scripture. You may want to add more questions or skip some according to your own family's needs. If you do not have children in one of the age groups mentioned in the study, do those questions anyway as they lend to the sequence of the lesson.

The prayer time can be augmented by prayer requests and varied in manner. The suggested prayer is given only as a guideline. It is important that your family realizes the significance of a powerful personal prayer life. Your time of prayer as a family should be an important part of your devotions and should be related to each of your own individual and family needs.

May God richly bless your family as you study his Word and join hearts in prayer together.

Introduction to the Book of Mark

The Book of Mark was written according to early tradition by John Mark about 65 A.D. It is the earliest record of the life of Jesus.

Mark, the author of this Gospel, was a nephew of Barnabas, and set out with Paul and Barnabas on their first missionary journey, as told in the Book of Acts. Upon reaching Perga, however, Mark left them and returned home (Acts 13:12). Later, Paul and Barnabas parted company when Paul refused to take Mark with them on a second missionary journey. The next time we read of Mark, however, is in Colossians where Paul mentions him as being a fellow prisoner. Paul also mentions him as a fellow laborer in Colossians 4:10 and 2 Timothy 4:11.

The Book of Mark is reported to be a collection of the observations and teachings of the Apostle Peter who was with Jesus and saw and heard everything firsthand.

Mark tells about Jesus in a simple, picturesque manner. He portrays Jesus as a compassionate, involved, and very human Savior.

Mark's Gospel was written to Christians with the intention of teaching them, through the life of Christ, the principles and values upon which they were to base their Christianity. It was also written as a means of encouragement for the Christians who were faced with both strong temptations and even possible martyrdom. The Book of Mark is as applicable today as it was then, just as Jesus is as powerful in our lives now as he was in the lives of the early Christians.

MARK 1:1-4

Open your devotional time by discussing any prayer requests that you as a family may have. If you help to support a missionary or know of a needy person or family, you'll want to suggest them also. Discuss things that you as a family can praise the Lord for. Now take these things to God in prayer.

Read Mark 1:1-4.

Child: 1. What was the name of God's special messenger?
2. Did he come before or after Jesus?
3. Where did he live?

Teen: 1. What did the prophets foretell about John the Baptist?
2. Why did John the Baptist teach that all should be baptized?
3. What did John the Baptist demand of people before they could be baptized?
4. What does baptism mean to you?

Adult: 1. Repentance should be followed by a change of conduct. Are there any things in our family that should be confessed? Any changes that should be made as a result of these confessions?

Close in prayer asking Jesus to forgive any sin in your lives and ask him to help you turn your back on that sin. Thank him for his power to forgive your sins and for his love.

MARK 1:5-8

Begin by asking each member of your family to suggest something that he or she would like to do today to help some other family member. Then ask God to prepare your hearts for the study of his Word.

Read Mark 1:5-8.

Child: 1. Where did John baptize those who had confessed their sins?
2. Tell about the clothes John wore and the food he ate. How was John different from you?

Teen: 1. Who is John talking about in verse 7?
2. How does John compare himself with Jesus?
3. Discuss ways in which your being humble can be a means of bringing another person to know Christ.

Adult: 1. How did John compare the baptism that he gave with the baptism that Christ would give?
2. Discuss John's top priority or purpose in life as compared with your own. How can your purpose in life be one that brings glory to God and leads others to know Jesus?

Close in prayer dedicating your lives to Jesus and asking for his direction in each of your lives. Ask him to forgive your sins and to fill your hearts with his Holy Spirit.

MARK 1:9-13

Have each member of the family take turns standing up while the rest of the family each says something that they like especially well about that person.

Now ask God's blessing on this study of his Word.

Read Mark 1:9-13.

Child: 1. What did Jesus see after he was baptized?

        2. What did the voice from heaven say to Jesus?

        3. How do you feel when someone is pleased with you?

Teen: 1. Up until now John baptized those who repented of their sins. Why do you think that Jesus, the sinless one, chose to be baptized?

        2. What happened to Jesus immediately after he received the blessing of God's Holy Spirit?

Adult: 1. Matthew 4:1-11 gives a more detailed account of Jesus' temptation in the wilderness. How does Jesus withstand Satan's temptations?

        2. Who was there to care for Jesus during this time of testing? (Mark 1:13, Matthew 4:11)

        3. How can the Bible and the Holy Spirit help each of us through times of testing and temptation?

Join your hearts in prayer asking for God's help in times of testing and temptation. Ask him to fill you with his Spirit and his love, and thank him for being your Lord and Savior.

MARK 1:14–20

Discuss the different ways that your family gets the news. The gospel is called God's Good News for man. Let's see how this news was spread in Jesus' day.

Read Mark 1:14–20.

Child: 1. How did Jesus help others hear the Good News that he wanted them to hear?

2. How can you help to bring the Good News of Jesus' love to your friends?

Teen: 1. What two things did Jesus ask the people to do? (v. 15)

2. Jesus chose Simon, Andrew, James, and John to be his followers and later his disciples. What do you know about them from these verses?

Adult: 1. What were some of the things necessary to be left behind by the people whom Jesus chose as his followers?

2. Why do you think these followers of Jesus left everything so willingly to follow him?

3. How would you feel about changing your life's occupation or leaving behind loved ones to follow Jesus?

4. What things do you sometimes have to sacrifice in order to win others to the Lord?

Close in prayer thanking the Lord for all your earthly possessions and positions whatever they may be. Ask him to help you not to value these things more highly than his love and the opportunity and ability to share that love with those around you.

MARK 1:21-28

Children like to do things to prove that they are strong. Some children are very good at helping their moms and dads. Some are good runners, readers, or swimmers. Some can sing well, and some feel they can cry louder or fight better than anyone else. What do you feel that you do best?

Many people followed Jesus and listened to him because they knew that his strength and power were much greater than any they had ever seen before.

Read Mark 1:21-28.

Child: 1. What kind of man was interrupting the lesson Jesus was teaching?
        2. How did Jesus show the people his power?

Teen: 1. How was Jesus' teaching different from that of the others the people were used to? (v. 22)
        2. What does this tell you about Jesus?

Adult: 1. What two commands did Jesus give the demons?
        2. What was the people's reaction to the fact that the demons obeyed his commands?
        3. How did this increase Jesus' popularity?

Close in prayer thanking God for the power that Jesus has in our lives. Thank him too for his love and that he can transform our lives into lives that are pleasing to him.

MARK 1:29–34

Discuss a time in your life when you were feeling sick or hurt or your feelings were hurt and someone came to comfort you or make you feel better. How did you feel toward that person? Let's see how Jesus took care of others and how they responded to his love.

Read Mark 1:29–34.

Child: 1. What did Jesus do as soon as he heard that Simon's mother-in-law was sick?

2. What did the woman do as soon as she was well?

Teen: 1. How do we know from verse 30 that Jesus' disciples had learned to go to him for help?

2. When you are faced with a problem, do you take it to Jesus expecting him to help you?

Adult: 1. How did the fact that Jesus performed miracles affect the people of Galilee?

2. Why do you think that Jesus performed all these miracles?

Ask your family if there is anyone or anything special they would like to pray for. Close in prayer remembering these requests. Thank Jesus for his power and ability to perform miracles even in our lives today. Ask him to help you to remember to take your problems to him immediately, expecting him to answer.

MARK 1:35-39

Have you ever been interrupted while in the middle of a good conversation or an enjoyable time with someone special? Why is it important to spend time alone with others? Who in your family would you like to have more time alone with?

Read Mark 1:35-39.

Child: 1. When did Jesus find time to talk to his Father?
2. Where did Jesus go to pray?
3. Do you sometimes talk to God all by yourself?

Teen: 1. Is it sometimes difficult for you to find a time and place to be alone to talk to God?
2. What time and place are best for you to have a quiet time with God?
3. Why do you think this was so important to Jesus at this time?

Adult: 1. What did Jesus set forth as his purpose in verse 38?
2. What option did his disciples place before him?
3. Why is it easy for us to stay with those who are familiar to us and not reach out to new souls sharing with them the gospel message?

Close in prayer thanking the Lord for the times shared alone with each other, getting to know and love one another. Thank him for prayer and the opportunity we have to be alone with him in order to draw close to him and know his love and power in our lives. Ask him for forgiveness for the times when you have become too busy or neglectful of this special privilege.

MARK 1:40-45

Have you ever felt very sorry for someone when everyone else was against that person? Have you ever befriended someone that everyone else disliked even though you thought others might make fun of you or dislike you too because you cared about this person? Do you know someone now who needs special love and attention?

Read Mark 1:40-45.

Child: 1. How do you think Jesus felt toward the leper?
2. How soon was the leper healed?
3. What does this tell you about Jesus?
4. What should your attitude be toward those that are unlovely?

Teen: 1. What was the attitude of the leper when he came to Jesus?
2. Do you think the leper felt that he in any way deserved God's mercy?
3. What can be learned about the power of Jesus through these verses?

Adult: 1. Jesus insisted that the leper adhere to the Law by going to the priest following his healing (Lev. 13: 1-3; 14:1). What do you think was Jesus' attitude toward the law in this instance?
2. What do you think caused the leper to disobey Jesus?
3. What were the results of his disobedience?

Close in prayer praising God for his love, his compassion, his power, his forgiveness, and his healing within and without.

MARK 2:1–12

Ask each member of your family to name something specific that he would like to ask God for, either for himself or someone else, either spiritual, physical, or material. Pray a short prayer after each request in faith believing that God will answer that prayer.

Read Mark 2:1–12.

Child:
1. Under what conditions was Jesus preaching?
2. What did the four men who were carrying the sick man have to do to get him before Jesus?
3. What does that tell you about those men?

Teen:
1. How did Jesus begin his cure of the sick man?
2. Jesus knew that the people of that day believed that if you were sick you had probably sinned. Why do you think Jesus chose to forgive the man's sins before healing him?
3. What does this tell you about the wisdom of Jesus?

Adult:
1. What bothered the scribes about Jesus' ability to forgive sins?
2. What was Jesus' answer?
3. How do you think this affected the onlookers?
4. Examine the depth of your own faith in Jesus' ability to answer prayer.

Close in prayer asking God for forgiveness for any lack of faith in his ability to answer all your prayers. Thank him for the many times he has answered your prayers in the past. Ask him to lead you to people who need to be "carried" to Jesus.

MARK 2:13-17

Have you ever felt jealous or envious of the special attention that another person was getting because he especially needed it at that time? Perhaps the person was being disobedient and needed correction. Or maybe he was hurt and needed special care. How should we feel at these times?

Read Mark 2:13-17.

Child:
1. Whom did Jesus meet as he was walking up the beach?
2. What did he ask Levi, later called Matthew, to do?
3. What did Levi do?
4. Do you think it was easy for Levi to obey Jesus?

Teen:
1. What type of people did Levi associate with?
2. What do we know about Levi from his desire to share Jesus with his friends?
3. How do you feel about telling your friends about your relationship with Jesus?

Adult:
1. What were the scribes and Pharisees complaining about?
2. How did Jesus answer them?
3. How willing are you to associate with those who believe differently from you in order to win them to Jesus?
4. When was the last time you reached out to meet someone's need or really cared for someone though you felt he was "not your type" and you might face unfounded criticism by others for doing so?

Close in prayer asking the Lord to help you in sharing your faith in Christ with others. Ask him to help you make an extra effort to reach out and care about someone in order to show them his love.

MARK 2:18-22

Describe a time in your life when you were having a very good time or an interesting conversation with a good friend and you were interrupted by a request to perform some responsibility or obligation. Perhaps you felt that those obligations could wait until later since you had such a short time to spend with your friend. Let's see how Jesus and his disciples felt as they spent Jesus' last few days together.

Read Mark 2:18-22.

Child: 1. What was the religious habit of John's disciples and the Pharisees (Jewish leaders)?

2. What question did they ask Jesus?

3. How did Jesus answer their question (v. 19)?

Teen: 1. How did Jesus predict the disciples would act when he left them?

2. What do these verses say to you about the relationship between Jesus and his disciples?

Adult: 1. With what two things did Jesus compare the old Jewish habit of fasting?*

2. What was Jesus saying about the ability of people to accept new truth?

3. How flexible are you? How willing are you to make adjustments in your life in order to accept that which is new or unfamiliar to you?

Close in prayer asking God for a heart that is open and cleansed and filled with his Holy Spirit.

*Sewing new cloth on old caused a problem because the new cloth would shrink, causing the old cloth to tear.

The old skins that were used to store wine became stiff and unyielding with age. New wine would give off gases as it fermented and would cause the old bottles, incapable of expanding, to explode.

MARK 2:23–28

Describe a special time in your life when your usual habits were temporarily changed to meet your need—perhaps you were allowed to stay up later than usual because it was a special evening or your family decided to take a different road than usual in order to get some ice cream. How did you feel at that time?

Read Mark 2:23–28.

Child:
1. Where were the people walking?
2. What day of the week was it?
3. What were Jesus' disciples doing?

Teen:
1. What were the Pharisees complaining about?
2. What do you think the Pharisees expected Jesus to do?
3. What was Jesus' answer?
4. How do these verses show Jesus' love for his disciples?

Adult:
1. Jesus cites here the story told about David in 1 Samuel 21:1-6. What reason does he give for the disciples breaking the law of the Sabbath?
2. How do Jesus' words in verse 27 help us to realize that he valued mankind far more highly than petty rules and regulations?
3. Discuss how easy it is to get caught up in obeying rules and regulations and forget about the needs of those around us.
4. What did Jesus say about himself in verse 28?

Close in prayer thanking Jesus for his love for you. Ask him to help you love others and always be alert to recognizing their needs. Ask him to teach you how to be obedient to him without feeling like you are "required to obey."

MARK 3:1-6

Have you ever sensed that someone needed you and yet you did nothing about it? How did you feel afterwards? Describe a time when you met someone's need (were a friend, made a visit, took food or clothing, invited someone to Sunday School, gave up something for someone). Can you think of someone today that your family can pray for and perhaps help?

Read Mark 3:1-6.

Child: 1. Where did Jesus go?

2. What day of the week was it?

3. The Jewish leaders had very strict rules about what they were allowed to do on the Sabbath day. They were not allowed to do anything that could possibly wait until the next day. What did Jesus want to do?

4. What did Jesus value more than rules?

Teen: 1. What is the attitude of Jesus' enemies now?

2. What two questions did Jesus ask them?

3. Why do you think they refused to answer him?

Adult: 1. What was Jesus' attitude toward the Sabbath?

2. What emotions did Jesus feel at this time?

3. What was the difference between the Pharisees' religion and Jesus' teaching?

4. How does this same situation occur in our churches today?

Take time to pray for specific people with needs such as were mentioned in the beginning of this lesson. Ask the Lord to help you to love others and be more concerned for them and their needs. Ask God to help you to use every day to his glory.

MARK 3:7-12

What does the word *popular* mean? Have you ever been in a situation in which you were popular? How important is it to you to be popular?

Read Mark 3:7-12.

Child:
1. How popular was Jesus?
2. What did Jesus have waiting for him in case he was overcome by the crowd?
3. Why did so many people come to Jesus?

Teen:
1. Do you think Jesus was impressed by his own popularity?
2. What do you think was most important to Jesus?
3. How can this apply to you?

Adult:
1. What did the unclean spirits recognize about Jesus?
2. What did Jesus say to them?
3. Why do you think Jesus wanted the unclean spirits' message quieted at this time?

Close in prayer thanking Jesus for his love and for being your Savior. If you have never invited him into your heart, do it today! Ask him to help you to value his love and the sharing of that love more than your own popularity with others.

MARK 3:13-19

Take turns discussing a time when you were chosen to do a special job for someone or chosen above everyone else for a special responsibility (babysitting, washing the blackboards for a teacher, being the first in line, etc.). How did you feel at that time?

Read Mark 3:13-19.

Child: 1. Where did Jesus go?

        2. How many disciples did Jesus invite to go with him?

        3. How do you think these disciples felt when Jesus chose them out of all the others to go with him and be his disciples?

Teen: 1. Read the names that Jesus gave to his disciples. To which disciples did he give special names?

        2. How do we usually feel about those to whom we give special nicknames?

        3. Which disciple did Jesus name last?

Adult: 1. What were the responsibilities that Jesus gave to his disciples?

        2. Judging by worldly standards, did these disciples have any special talents or abilities that would cause them to be especially qualified for these tasks?

        3. What reasons do you think Jesus may have had for choosing these particular men to be his special disciples?

Close in prayer thanking Jesus that he has called us to be his "disciples"—to love and care for others and to bring his gospel message to those who need to hear it. Ask him to help you to be faithful in carrying out your special responsibilities for him.

MARK 3:20–30

Have you ever been accused of doing something that you knew you didn't do? Were you able to convince your accuser of your innocence in the matter?

Let's see how Jesus was accused falsely and how he wisely defended himself in this lesson.

Read Mark 3:20–30.

Child: 1. What did Jesus' friends say about him in verse 21?
2. Why did they say that?
3. What didn't they understand about Jesus?

Teen: 1. Of what did the scribes accuse Jesus?
2. How did Jesus answer them (v. 23)?
3. What examples did he give them to further illustrate his point?
4. Who is the strong man that Jesus referred to in verse 27?

Adult: 1. What did Jesus say about forgiveness in verse 28?
2. What is the one sin that cannot be forgiven?
3. How did the scribes in this lesson blaspheme the Holy Spirit?

Close in prayer thanking Jesus for his wisdom in dealing with people. Thank him for giving you wisdom and ask him to help you to call on his wisdom always in your relationships with others. Thank God that the power of the Holy Spirit within you can defeat satanic forces whenever you call upon him to do so.

MARK 3:31-35

Take turns naming some qualities that are important in order to be a responsible family member (example: loyalty, thoughtfulness, concern, etc.). What kinds of attitudes would you like to see more of in your home?

Read Mark 3:31-35.

Child: 1. Who came to where Jesus was teaching?
2. Where did they stand?
3. What did they want Jesus to do?

Teen: 1. What did Jesus ask the crowd in verse 33?
2. What answer do you think Jesus expected from the crowd?
3. Do you think they were surprised by his answer in verse 34?

Adult: 1. Who do you think was part of his family?
2. What do you think was Jesus' attitude toward his mother and brothers at this time?
3. How can we become part of God's family?

Close in prayer thanking God for being your heavenly Father and for making you a part of his family. Ask him to help you to be a faithful member both to your family on earth and, as a child of God, to your heavenly family.

MARK 4:1–20

Have you ever heard someone's voice speaking but not actually heard what they were saying? Did you ever have trouble following instructions because you did not listen carefully when they were given? In this lesson Jesus tells a story about the importance of listening carefully and following the instructions in God's Word.

Read Mark 4:1–20.

Child:
1. Where did Jesus go this time to teach the people? Why?
2. What is the farmer doing in verse 3?
3. What does Jesus tell you to do in verse 9?

Teen:
1. Read verses 4 and 15. Describe what happens to seed that falls on hard ground. What did Jesus liken it to?
2. Read verses 5-6 and 16-17. What happens to seed that falls on rocky soil? With what kind of person did Jesus compare this?
3. Read verses 7, 18, and 19. What happens when seed falls on thorny ground? How did Jesus compare this to some people's hearts?
4. Read verses 8 and 20. What happens to seed that falls on good soil? What type of heart does this represent?

Adult:
1. What things have you allowed to stunt your growth as a Christian?
2. Describe again what happens to the person who allows God's Word to take root in his heart (v. 20).

3. Read Galatians 5:22-23. Are you a fruit-bearing, harvest-producing Christian?

Close in prayer asking God to prepare your hearts to hear his word and to follow the instructions written there. Ask him to cleanse you and fill your heart with his love and with his Spirit.

MARK 4:21–25

Take turns mentioning something good that each member of your family has done for someone else in the family during the past week. Doing these loving, helpful things for others is a way of showing our love for Jesus.

Read Mark 4:21–25.

Child: 1. What is a candle or lamp used for?
      2. What doesn't a person do with a lamp? Why?
      3. Read Matthew 5:16. How can we let the light of God's presence in our hearts shine for him?

Teen: 1. What did Jesus say will happen when a person tries to hide something (v. 22)?
      2. If you truly believe in Jesus Christ as your Savior and your Lord, is it possible to keep it a secret?

Adult: 1. What did Jesus say will happen when we put what we hear into practice (v. 24)?
      2. What happens when you do not use a talent for a long period of time?
      3. What did Jesus say will happen if you do not put into practice what you have learned from his word (v. 25)?

Close in prayer thanking God for his Word that teaches us how to live lives that please him. Ask him to help you practice daily what you learn. Ask that he may help you never have to attempt to "hide" anything from friends or God. Pray that your life may shine to his glory.

MARK 4:26–34

Take turns describing something which began very small but with lots of people's help grew very large—for example, some of you may know the story "Stone Soup"; other examples could be a Sunday School class, a nation, a new building, even a quilt that is made with many ladies adding a block. Jesus described his kingdom for us in much the same way.

Read Mark 4:26–34.

Child: 1.   What did the man do in verse 26?
       2.   What happened to the seed that was planted?
       3.   What did the farmer do after the grain had fully grown?

Teen: 1.   What things do verses 26-29 tell you about God's Kingdom?
       2.   How does Jesus describe his Kingdom in verses 30-32?

Adult: 1.   Who do you think the birds represent in verse 32?
       2.   Who belongs in God's Kingdom?
       3.   How do you know from verse 33 that Jesus was a good teacher?
       4.   What does verse 34 tell about the special relationship between Jesus and his disciples?

Close in prayer thanking Jesus for making you a part of his Kingdom. Pray today especially for all those who are involved in leadership in your place of worship. Pray for all those who work in God's Kingdom.

MARK 4:35-41

A family goes through many "storms" in life both together and as individuals. Take turns naming some of the "storms" (arguments, problems, fears, sorrows, etc.) that you have encountered along life's way. Let's see now how Jesus brings calm to the storm.

Read Mark 4:35-41.

Child: 1. What did Jesus and his disciples decide to do (v. 35)?
2. Describe the storm that occurred when Jesus and his disciples were out on the water.
3. Have you ever felt very frightened during a rain storm?
4. What did you do when you were frightened?

Teen: 1. Where was Jesus during the storm?
2. What was the disciples reaction to the fact that Jesus was sleeping during the storm?
3. What did Jesus immediately do to the storm?
4. How did he feel about the disciples' lack of confidence in him?

Adult: 1. Read 1 Peter 5:7. What does God expect us to do in the stormy times of life?
2. How did the disciples feel when they saw how Jesus calmed the storm?
3. Why would this miracle mean more to the disciples than any of the other miracles they had seen Jesus perform?
4. How should the disciples have been able to face future storms?

Close in prayer thanking God that he gives peace in the stormy times of our lives. Ask him to help you trust him fully to meet your needs, calm your fears, and give you strength and courage to meet any problems that face you. If you know anyone who is now having trouble, pray for them.

MARK 5:1-20

Discuss a time when you were separated from a loved one because of illness. How did you feel at that time?

Read Mark 5:1-20.

Child:
1. What was the condition of the man who ran out to meet Jesus as he came to the other side of the lake?
2. What did Jesus do for the man?
3. What did Jesus tell the man to do for him (v. 19)?
4. Jesus has done many things for us. How can we show our love for him?

Teen:
1. What things did the evil spirits recognize about Jesus?
2. Name some of the changes that took place in the possessed man when he was cured.
3. What did the changes tell about Jesus' power?

Adult:
1. What was the people's reaction to this healing?
2. Why do you think they reacted that way?
3. How did the healed man show his gratitude toward Jesus (vv. 18-20)?

Close in prayer thanking God for your health and for the joy of being together with those who are dear to you. Ask him to help you to appreciate and to be considerate of those in your home and of your friends and relatives that are often taken for granted.

MARK 5:21-24, 35-43

Have you ever felt sad or discouraged when no one seemed to understand how bad you felt? Maybe there were many cloudy days in a row and you thought the sun was never going to shine again. Maybe you had an injury or illness, and it seemed like you would never be well. We need to be like the man in this lesson and turn our problems over to Jesus.

Read Mark 5:21-24, 35-43.

Child:
1. Who was Jairus?
2. What did he want Jesus to do?
3. How did he ask Jesus for this?

Teen:
1. What message came to Jesus while he was on his way to Jairus's daughter?
2. How did Jesus reassure Jairus (v. 36)?
3. What does this tell you about Jesus' confidence in his power to heal? What does it tell you about his understanding of how Jairus must have felt?

Adult:
1. What situation was Jesus met with in verse 38?
2. How did the people react to Jesus' statement that Jairus's daughter was only sleeping?
3. How did Jesus cope with their scorn and unbelief?
4. How do you think the parents must have felt when their daughter was returned to life?
5. Discuss the reasons behind the two commands that Jesus gives in verse 43.

Close in prayer thanking Jesus for his concern for all our needs —spiritual, emotional and physical. Thank him for his power and ability to meet each of our needs. Ask him for the faith to trust him daily with each problem that you face.

MARK 5:25-34

Describe a time in your life when you had a problem and tried but were unable to solve it yourself. How did you feel when you finally found someone who had the answer to your problem or was able to help you?

Read Mark 5:25-34.

Child:
1. How long had the woman in this lesson been sick?
2. What did the sick woman try before coming to Jesus?
3. What happened to her when she tried going to doctors for help (v. 26)?
4. What did Jesus do for her?

Teen:
1. What do you know about the persistence of this woman in trying to solve her problem?
2. What did the woman know about Jesus?
3. What happened to Jesus when the woman touched him?
4. How did the disciples react when Jesus told them that someone had touched him?

Adult:
1. Read Leviticus 15:25-27. According to Jewish laws this woman was unclean; anyone who touched her would also be declared unclean. (That is why she approached Jesus in the manner described). Tell how the woman must have felt in verse 33.
2. What does Jesus say was the reason he healed her?

Take turns today naming something that each of you has to be thankful for. Now take turns praising God for these things.

MARK 6:1-6

Discuss how you would feel if someone that you felt very close to (perhaps a sister or brother) suddenly became famous. Knowing so much about him, would you be as much in awe of him as the rest of the world? Have you ever felt that those in your own family do not pay as much attention to you as those outside your family?

Read Mark 6:1-6.

Child: 1. To where did Jesus return(v. 1)?
2. What did the people think of Jesus' preaching and miracles?

Teen: 1. What astounded the people the most about Jesus?
2. Why do you think this offended them?

Adult: 1. What did Jesus say about people's reactions to those in their own family who are successful?
2. How can we keep this from happening?
3. How did the people's lack of faith hinder Jesus' work in this town (v. 5)?

Take turns naming something that each of you has to be thankful for about another person in your family. Close in prayer thanking God for each person in your family and for the ways in which God has blessed you. Ask him to help you to truly love and appreciate one another.

MARK 6:7–13

Did you ever hear the old adage "divide and conquer"? Name some times when your family has divided the responsibilities and cooperated in order to complete a certain task (for example: planning and gathering things for a picnic, carrying things from the car to the beach, cleaning up a room, etc.).

Read Mark 6:7–13.
Child: 1. How many disciples did Jesus send out to tell others about him?
          2. How did he send them out?
          3. What reasons do you think Jesus may have had for sending the disciples out by twos?
Teen: 1. What orders did Jesus give the twelve disciples?
          2. What reasons do you think Jesus had for giving each of these orders?
          3. What do we learn about self-denial from these verses?
Adult: 1. What was the message that the disciples preached?
          2. What additional means did the disciples use to carry Christ's message?
          3. How did dividing and sending out the disciples help to further the spread of the Gospel?

Close in prayer thanking Jesus for the power of the Holy Spirit in your lives. Ask him to make you willing to be his disciple and help with the task of telling others about him.

MARK 6:14-29

Describe a time when you have admired something that someone else has done or become, but lacked the courage, discipline, or self-denial to do the same yourself. (Make an effort to be honest with yourself about this moment of confession.)

Read Mark 6:14-29.

Child: 1. Who did King Herod think Jesus was (v. 14)?
      2. Who did some of the other people think that Jesus was (v. 15)?

Teen: 1. Why did King Herod have John the Baptist put in prison (vv. 16-18)?
      2. Why was Herodias, King Herod's wife, powerless to have John the Baptist killed (v. 19)?
      3. How did Herodias manage to trick King Herod into killing John the Baptist?

Adult: 1. What was Herodias's basic sin?
      2. What was King Herod's basic sin?
      3. Why did King Herod fail to believe what John had to say even though he respected and approved of John?

Close in prayer thanking Jesus that he is the Lord and Savior of your life. Thank him that he can do through you that which is impossible for you to do on your own. Ask him to make you willing to daily yield to him. Ask God to give you the courage to accept the success of others, and to accept criticism of yourself gracefully in Christian love.

MARK 6:30–44

Describe a time when you made plans and had them interrupted or ruined because someone needed you or wanted you to do something else. How did you feel at that time? Let's see how Jesus and his disciples made some plans and had them interrupted by a needy crowd of people.

Read Mark 6:30–44.

Child: 1. Describe the miracle that Jesus performed. (You might like to try acting it out.)
2. How much food was left over after the people were finished eating (vv. 43, 44)?
3. What does this tell you about how Jesus takes care of our needs?

Teen: 1. What did Jesus and his apostles need to do (v. 31)?
2. How and where were they going to get the rest they needed?
3. What happened to interrupt the plans they had made (v. 33)?
4. How did Jesus feel toward the crowd that had interrupted his plans?

Adult: 1. How do you react when others interrupt your need for rest or privacy?
2. What problem did the disciples bring to Jesus and how did they suggest handling it (vv. 35, 36)?
3. How do you think the disciples felt physically by this time?
4. What was Jesus' answer to their problem (v. 37)?
5. Do you think the disciples shared Christ's feeling of compassion for the multitude?

Close in prayer thanking Jesus for his loving understanding of our needs. Thank him for the way he has met your needs. Ask him for compassion for those whose needs you are required to meet. Pray for special love and understanding for someone you feel needs it today.

MARK 6:45-56

Describe a time when you felt very frightened. How did you overcome your fear? Let's look now at a frightening experience that the disciples had and see how their fears were calmed.

Read Mark 6:45-56.

Child:
1. What happened to the disciples as they were out in their boat?
2. What did Jesus do (v. 46)?
3. What did they think Jesus was?
4. How did Jesus calm their fears (vv. 50, 51)?
5. You might enjoy acting out this story.

Teen:
1. Why did Jesus remain on land?
2. Note Jesus' need for communication with the source of his strength and power. How does this apply to you?
3. Where did Jesus go to pray? Why?

Adult:
1. What does verse 52 say about the disciples?
2. What kind of reception did Jesus get at Gennesaret?
3. What was the reason for his popularity there?

Close in prayer thanking Jesus for his love and power. Ask him for forgiveness for times of unbelief. Bring any fears that you have to him and ask him to help you to trust in him and not be afraid.

MARK 7:1–13

Name some things that by the way they look on the outside can fool people (for example: books, houses, people, etc.).

Let's see what Jesus thought about the scribes and Pharisees as they kept all the rules and regulations but forgot to love God and those around them.

Read Mark 7:1–13.

Child: 1. What did the Jews always do before eating (vv. 3, 4)?
2. What didn't the disciples do?
3. To whom did the Pharisees complain?

Teen: 1. What did Jesus call the Pharisees (v. 6)?
2. Look up the word *hypocrite* in the dictionary. What does it mean?
3. In what ways are people hypocrites today?

Adult: 1. What did Jesus say about the worship of the Jews?
2. What example does Jesus use to show how the Jews were living in opposition to the truth? (The word *corban* meant "dedicated to God." The Jews could dedicate their money or property to God and thus evade taking care of their needy parents.)
3. What was the Pharisees' criteria for judging their righteousness?
4. How does God judge a person's righteousness?

Close in prayer thanking God for your salvation through Jesus Christ. Thank him that it is not by works of our own that we are saved, but by his mercy and love. Ask his forgiveness for times of hypocrisy and ask him to help you to be a loving example of the fact that he lives in your heart.

MARK 7:14-23

Have you ever been told, "Now listen carefully because I want to be *sure* you understand what I'm saying"? Under what circumstances might it be most important that you listen?

Read Mark 7:14-23.

Child: 1. What two commands did Jesus give to the crowd to show them that what he had to say was important (v. 14)?

2. Why do you think it was so important to Jesus that the crowd hear these particular words of warning?

Teen: 1. The Pharisees had a long list of foods which they considered unclean, and they were not allowed to eat them. What did Jesus say was more harmful than eating the wrong foods (vv. 15, 20)?

2. Why could what you think and say be more harmful than the food you eat?

Adult: 1. Name and define the things that Jesus says defile a man.

2. How does a person rid himself of these defilements?

Close in prayer thanking Jesus for his power to forgive sin. Ask him for forgiveness for any sin in your lives that your hearts may be pure and fit for him to use.

MARK 7:24-30

Discuss a time when someone was reluctant to give you something that you wanted very much. How did you go about convincing them that you deserved the thing that you desired?

Read Mark 7:24-30.
Child: 1. Where did Jesus go?
            2. What was he unable to do (v. 24)?
            3. Who came to Jesus for help?
Teen: 1. How did the woman ask Jesus for help?
            2. This woman was a Gentile who was declared unclean by the Jews whom Jesus refers to as the children in this portion of Scripture (v. 27). What did Jesus say to the woman?
Adult: 1. How did the woman answer Jesus?
            2. Why do you think Jesus was pleased with her answer?

Close in prayer thanking Jesus that his salvation and his answers to our prayers are for everyone who asks. Thank him that we don't have to deserve his love, but that his love is a gift for anyone who is willing to receive it.

MARK 7:31-37

Discuss how you feel when you know something very exciting that no one else knows, and you are expected to keep it a secret.

Read Mark 7:31-37.

Child: 1. Who was brought to Jesus and what did the people ask Jesus to do for him?

         2. Tell about how Jesus healed the man.

Teen: 1. Why do you think Jesus looked up to heaven before healing the man?

         2. What happened as soon as the man was healed (v. 35)?

Adult: 1. What request did Jesus make of the people?

         2. Why were they unable to obey his request?

Close in prayer thanking Jesus specifically for any answers to prayer that you have recently received. Ask him to fill your heart so much with thankfulness for all the blessings that you have recieved that it will be impossible for you to keep it a secret.

MARK 8:1-10

Take turns naming something that someone in your family could do for you today (example: sew a button, iron a shirt, mail a letter, carry out trash, etc.). Make sure no one is excluded from doing something for someone else in the family today.

Read Mark 8:1-10.

Child: 1. How long had the crowd been with Jesus? What did the crowd begin to feel?
2. How did Jesus react to the fact that the people were hungry?

Teen: 1. What was the disciples' reaction to the people's hunger?
2. Contrast the difference between Jesus and the disciples' compassion for the people's needs with the different reactions that people today have toward other people in need.

Adult: 1. Read Mark 6:30-44 again. What differences do you see in these two incidents?
2. How do you go about meeting the physical and spiritual needs of those around you?

Close in prayer thanking God for your family and your friends. Ask him to help you to be sensitive to the needs of others and willing to do whatever you can to help.

MARK 8:11-21

Discuss some of the ways that we see God's hand in our world every day. Do we need special signs or miracles to prove God's love for us?

Read Mark 8:11-21.

Child: 1. What did the Pharisees want Jesus to do (v. 11)?
2. Why was Jesus disappointed by their request?
3. Do you ever expect your parents to show their love by giving you things even though you see their love each day by the things they do for you?

Teen: 1. What did the disciples forget to take on the boat with them?
2. What was Jesus warning them to beware of? (The leaven in bread was a symbol of evil or sin.)
3. What are some of the sins of the Pharisees and Herod that Jesus was referring to (Mark 6-7; Luke 12:1)?

Adult: 1. How did the disciples misunderstand Jesus?
2. How did Jesus react to their misunderstanding?
3. How do we sometimes forget the good things that God has done for us in the past when we are faced with a problem?
4. How should the good things that God has done for us affect our relationship with him?

Take turns naming some of the good things that God has done for you. Thank him for these things. Ask him to help you remember these things when you are faced with a new problem. Ask him for faith that you might believe that he can control every situation in your life.

MARK 8:22-26

Discuss some of the things in life that come to you gradually rather than suddenly (example: education, maturity, etc.).

Read Mark 8:22-26.

Child:
1. Who came to Jesus for healing?
2. How did he get to Jesus?
3. How did the people that brought the blind man ask Jesus to heal him?
4. Do you remember how your mother's or father's touch would often make a sore feel better?

Teen:
1. What stages did the blind man go through in order to receive his sight?
2. What are some of the stages (experiences) you have gone through in order to receive the spiritual sight that you now have?

Adult:
1. Notice the variety that Jesus uses in each miracle that he performs.
2. Why do you think he varies his method of healing with each person that he deals with? How can this apply to you?

Close in prayer thanking Jesus that he loves us and recognizes our differences. Thank him for meeting our individual needs. Ask him for sensitivity to the uniqueness of those he calls you to witness to that you may reach them with his message.

MARK 8:27–33

Discuss a time when someone you considered a friend tried to persuade you to do something contrary to what you knew was right. How did you react to that person? How *should* you react in such a situation?

Read Mark 8:27–33.

Child: 1. What did Jesus ask his disciples as they were walking along?
2. What was the disciples' answer?
3. What was the next question Jesus asked the disciples?
4. What was their answer?

Teen: 1. If Jesus asked you these two questions today, how would you answer him?
2. What four things did Jesus say would happen to him?

Adult: 1. What was Peter's reaction to Jesus' predictions of what would happen to him?
2. Why do you think this disturbed Jesus?
3. Why do you think Peter reacted the way he did?

Close in prayer thanking Jesus that he loved you enough to suffer and die for you. Thank him for becoming your own personal Savior. Ask him to forgive you for any sin in your life and to help you to share his love with those around you. (Be specific as to which sins you are asking forgiveness. If you have never invited Christ into your heart, now would be a good time to ask him to enter!)

MARK 8:34–9:1

Discuss what it would be like if each person in your family lived only for his own comfort and happiness and gave nothing of himself for anyone else in the family. What would our world be like if doctors, scientists, inventors, and especially Christians were only concerned with living a life of ease?

Read Mark 8:34–9:1.

Child:
1. What two things did Jesus tell the crowd they must do in order to follow him?
2. What pleasures do you sometimes have to give up in order to follow Jesus?

Teen:
1. What attitude did Jesus say we should take toward our life (v. 35)?
2. What problems do you face in "losing your life" for Jesus' sake?
3. What other option does verse 35 say is open to you?

Adult:
1. What does verse 36 say about having worldly success as a major priority?
2. What do these verses say about the worth of a soul?
3. How do these verses affect your list of priorities?
4. What does Mark 9:1 say the disciples would see in their lifetime? (The Kingdom of God refers here to the body of Christ, his Church.)

Close in prayer thanking Jesus for the life he has given you. Ask him to take your life and use it to glorify him. Ask him to make you willing to deny any personal desires for pleasure and success that would hinder your life from promoting the furtherance of his gospel.

MARK 9:2-13

Describe a time when someone explained something to you that you were not ready or willing to accept. How did you react? How did you finally adjust to the truth?

Read Mark 9:2-13.

Child:
1. This event is called "the transfiguration." Describe what happened to Jesus at this time (vv. 2, 3).
2. Where was Jesus and who was with him when this occurred?
3. How do you think this event made Jesus seem to the disciples?

Teen:
1. Who else appeared on the scene and began talking with Jesus (v. 4)?
2. What was Peter's reaction to this overwhelming occurrence? Why do you think he reacted in this way (v. 6)?
3. The disciples were finding it very difficult to accept the idea of Jesus' forthcoming death and resurrection that he was explaining to them. Why do you think God's words (v. 7) were especially important at this time?

Adult:
1. What command did Jesus give the disciples as they were coming down from the mountain? For how long were they to keep this command?
2. What questions did the disciples have?
3. Matthew 17:12, 13 explains about Elijah by referring to John the Baptist. What did Jesus say about the suffering that he would go through?

Close in prayer thanking God for Jesus and what his earthly ministry has meant to us. Thank him for allowing Jesus, his only Son, to be born and raised as we are that we might identify with all that he went through for us. Ask him that we will remember his suffering when we suffer and know, as he did, that God's hand is in everything that happens to us.

MARK 9:14-29

Discuss a time when you were asked to do a job which seemed much too difficult for you to do. Maybe you started but lost faith in your ability to finish the job, and you turned to someone else for help. Let's see now how the disciples faced a similar problem.

Read Mark 9:14-29.

Child: 1. Describe the situation that Jesus met as he came down from the mountain.

         2. How bad was the boy's problem (vv. 18, 22)?

         3. How long had he had this problem (v. 21)?

Teen: 1. Why were the disciples unable to heal the boy?

         2. What is faith? (Read Hebrews 11:1 aloud.)

         3. Why did Jesus feel that this situation required prayer (v. 29)?

Adult: 1. Why do you think Jesus was beginning to lose patience (v. 19)?

         2. How did the boy's father react to Jesus' requirement for him to have faith (v. 24)?

         3. In what situations are faith and prayer necessary in our lives today?

Close in prayer thanking the Lord for his power and ability to work mightily in and through our lives. Ask him for faith to believe that through him all things are possible. Ask him to make that faith evident by the way you live your life.

MARK 9:30–37

Discuss what traits you feel you should have in order to be the greatest person in your family, school, church, or nation. Let's see what Jesus says it takes to be the greatest.

Read Mark 9:30–37.

Child:
1. Who did Jesus spend most of his time with in this lesson?
2. What did he find was of great importance to the disciples?
3. How are you sometimes like they were?
4. What did Jesus tell them it takes to be great (v. 35)?

Teen:
1. How did the disciples feel about telling Jesus that being great was important to them (v. 34)?
2. Why do you think they were ashamed to admit it?
3. What was Jesus' reaction to their desire for greatness?
4. Why did Jesus use a child to further illustrate his point?

Adult:
1. What was uppermost in Jesus' mind at this time (vv. 30, 31)?
2. How did the disciples react to his teachings about his coming death and resurrection (v. 32)?
3. In the light of these verses, how is it all the more disturbing to think that the disciples were so preoccupied with the idea of who would be greatest?
4. How does Jesus' death and resurrection show that he really understood the meaning of true greatness?
5. How does this lesson apply to you in your home, job, relationships with friends, church, etc.?

Close in prayer thanking Jesus for his death and resurrection and what it means to you. Thank him for being one whose greatness is to love and serve others. Ask him for a heart that's committed to loving and caring for others and for less desire for recognition for yourself.

MARK 9:38-50

Discuss a time when you felt that you did not want to allow someone to join your group, club, church, etc. because they thought, looked or acted differently from you.

Read Mark 9:38-50.

Child:
1. What complaint did John bring to Jesus (v. 38)?
2. How did Jesus answer John?
3. What does it mean to do things "in Jesus' name"?
4. Why is caring for others an important part of belonging to Jesus?

Teen:
1. What did Jesus say about our responsibility toward others (v. 42)?
2. What did Jesus say we should do if we are not able to control certain aspects of our lives (vv. 43-45)?
3. From time to time there are some habits, friends, pleasures that need to be "amputated" from our lives in order for us to be useful, productive Christians. Are there any areas of your life that need to be pruned?

Adult:
1. What did Jesus say in these verses about punishment?
2. What are some of the "dos and don'ts" in these verses that characterize a true follower of Jesus?
3. What does salt do? How does a Christian have the same effect as salt on those around them?

Take turns naming problem areas in your lives and then take turns praying for each other. Thank God for his power in your lives and for his ability to make you what he wants you to be.

MARK 10:1-12

Discuss the importance of choosing the right mate for your life. What are some difficulties encountered when a person chooses the wrong mate? How can you be sure you are making the right choice?

Read Mark 10:1-12.

Child: 1. What was the question the Pharisees asked Jesus?
2. What does *divorce* mean (v. 2)?
3. What problems do you think children from divorced parents face?

Teen: 1. Why did Moses allow divorce?
2. Why did God create male and female?
3. What did Jesus say happens when two people become man and wife (v. 8)?

Adult: 1. What sin is involved when someone divorces his spouse and marries another?
2. Why is it important that we have God's blessing on such a major decision as choosing a mate?
3. What alternatives to divorce are available to those who are unhappy in their marriage?

Close in prayer thanking God for his love and interest in every aspect of our lives. Ask him for guidance as you face major decisions, for love for each other in your home, and for his blessing as you seek his will in your relationships with others. Pray for those whose homes and families are now broken.

MARK 10:13–16

Have you ever approached a game or a project knowing nothing at all about it but feeling eager to learn? Jesus wants us to come to him in much the same way—not with intellectual knowledge but with a ready heart.

Read Mark 10:13–16.

Child: 1. Whom did mothers bring to Jesus? Why?
        2. What did the disciples think about this? Why?
        3. How do we know from these verses that Jesus loves children?

Teen: 1. How did Jesus feel toward his disciples when they tried to keep the children from bothering him?
        2. Why did Jesus feel that children were important?

Adult: 1. How does Jesus say we should receive him?
        2. What do you think he meant by this?
        3. How do attitudes of bitterness, judging, criticism, backbiting, etc., fit into this picture?

Close in prayer thanking Jesus for his acceptance and love for us irregardless of our age, education, color, personality, or even our sins. Ask him for the humility and simplicity of a child as we come to him with our needs and as we follow him in worship and in service.

MARK 10:17-31

Discuss a time when you wanted to have something very much but you were not willing to pay the price. See in this lesson how serious this can be in spiritual matters.

Read Mark 10:17-31.

Child:
1. What did the man in verse 17 ask Jesus?
2. What did Jesus first tell him (v. 19)?
3. How did Jesus feel toward this man (v. 21)?
4. What two things did Jesus tell the man he must do?

Teen:
1. Why was the man in this lesson unable to follow Jesus' instructions?
2. What did Jesus say about the rich entering his kingdom?
3. Why do you think rich people have more problems following Jesus than others?

Adult:
1. What did Jesus say about the rewards of sacrifice in order to follow him?
2. What do these verses say about establishing the right values?
3. What do these verses say about eternity (vv. 30, 31)?

Close in prayer thanking God for the blessings that he has bestowed upon you and your family. Ask him to help you to realize the difference between what is temporary and what is eternal and to help you to place your values on that which will be most lasting.

MARK 10:32-45

Describe a time when you didn't get a special position, honor, or special praise that you felt you deserved. How did you feel when you didn't receive it? Let's see what Jesus says is more important than honor or position.

Read Mark 10:32-45.

Child: 1. What was Jesus talking to the disciples about on the way to Jerusalem?
2. How did they react to this discussion (v. 32)?
3. What things did Jesus predict would happen to him?

Teen: 1. What favor did James and John ask of Jesus?
2. What did he ask them if they were willing to do?
3. What was their answer?
4. What was Jesus' final answer to their request?
5. Why do you think they wanted these special seats of honor?

Adult: 1. How did the other disciples react when they heard James's and John's request?
2. Why do you think this disturbed them?
3. What did Jesus say about greatness?
4. How did he show that he was an example of what he taught about greatness?

Close in prayer thanking Jesus for his death on the cross that we can know him and have eternal life. Ask him for the strength to follow his example of "greatness" which is to love and care for others.

MARK 10:46-52

Describe a time when you have been against something until someone you admired was for it (or vice versa). Perhaps you have been the one to influence someone else's opinions. Let's see how Jesus affected the attitudes of those around him.

Read Mark 10:46-52.
Child: 1.   Who was Bartimaeus?
         2.   What was he doing as Jesus was passing by?
         3.   What did he ask of Jesus?
Teen: 1.   How did the people react to Bartimaeus' loud cries for help?
         2.   Why do you think they were so indifferent to his need?
         3.   What did Bartimaeus do when the people tried to quiet him?
         4.   What do we know about him from his refusal to give up?
Adult: 1.   How did Jesus treat the blind beggar?
         2.   How did the crowd treat him when they saw that Jesus was going to help him?
         3.   Why do you think their attitude changed?
         4.   What did Jesus say was the reason for the blind man's being healed?
         5.   What did Bartimaeus do as soon as he was healed?

Close in prayer thanking Jesus for his mercy and his compassion for us. Ask him for faith that we might believe that he is able to answer all our prayers and supply all our needs. Ask him to help you as you express your thankfulness to him by following and living for him.

MARK 11:1–11

Have you ever had a time when you were worried about facing a situation in which you felt uneasy?

Jesus was returning to Jerusalem where his enemies awaited him. He rode triumphantly rather than secretively into the city and faced the crowds with confidence because he knew his message was right for them even though many of them refused to accept it.

Read Mark 11:1–11.

Child:
1. What did Jesus tell two of his disciples to do?
2. What were they suppose to say to anyone who asked what they were doing?
3. Where did they find the colt?
4. What was asked of the disciples, and what did they reply?
5. What amazing thing do these verses tell you about Jesus?

Teen:
1. What did the people do as the colt was brought to Jesus and as he rode to Jerusalem?
2. What did they say?
3. What was their feeling for him at that time?

Adult:
1. What kind of king did the people expect Jesus to become?
2. What did Jesus do when he got to Jerusalem?
3. What do these verses say about Jesus' attitude toward the future even though he knew what awaited him?

Close in prayer thanking Jesus for the confidence that we have when we face life with him in our hearts. Ask him for complete trust in his ability to control every situation in your life. Ask him to teach you how to obey him in all of your personal affairs, and ask him to be Lord of your life.

MARK 11:12–14, 20–26

Name some ways in which you see God in control every day (example: the rising and setting of the sun, the growth of flowers, etc.).

One of the lessons we learn from the following parable is the power of God over all things in the universe. Let's see now what Jesus says about how we as Christians can have God's power in our lives.

Read Mark 11:12–14, 20–26.

Child:
1. What did Jesus notice about the fig tree?
2. What did Jesus say to the tree?
3. Who heard him say it?
4. What did the disciples notice about the fig tree as they walked by it the next day (v. 20)?
5. What does this parable tell you about Jesus' power?

Teen:
1. What did Jesus tell the disciples they would be able to do?
2. What requirement had to be met before they could do these things?
3. Why are believers so often unable to live a powerful Christian life?
4. What excuses do we use instead of allowing Christ to fill our lives and work through us?

Adult:
1. What did Jesus say you should do while you are praying (v. 25)?
2. Have you ever held a grudge against anyone for a long period of time?
3. How does holding a grudge against someone affect your prayer life?
4. Why does Jesus say we should forgive others?

Close in prayer thanking God for his power over the universe as well as in each of our lives. Ask him to help you to yield to him so that his power can work through you to win others to him.

MARK 11:15–19, 27–33

Discuss a time when someone took something that meant a lot to you and used it for something other than what it was intended. Let's see how Jesus reacted on a similar occasion.

Read Mark 11:15–19, 27–33.

Child: 1. Where did Jesus go when he and his disciples returned to Jerusalem after spending the night in Bethany?

          2. Read verse 11. How do we know the temple was a very special place to Jesus?

          3. For what purpose is God's house intended?

Teen: 1. What did Jesus find happening in the temple?

          2. How did he react to this desecration?

          3. What did Jesus say his house is to be used for?

          4. How did the Jewish priests and leaders react when they heard what he had done?

Adult: 1. Who approached Jesus as he entered the temple the next day?

          2. What question did they ask him? Why?

          3. With what question did Jesus reply?

          4. Why were they afraid to answer his question?

Close in prayer thanking God for the privilege of worshiping him wherever, whenever, and however we please. Ask him to help you to remember to respect his house and to enjoy it as you use it to further your relationship with him and his people.

MARK 12:1–12

Describe a time when you were trusted with a responsibility and failed to carry it out. Were you punished for your failure? Do you feel you deserved this punishment?

Read Mark 12:1–12.

Child:
1. What did the man in the story do (v. 1)?
2. Why did the man send one of his servants back?
3. What did the men in charge of the vineyard do to the servant?
4. What happened to the next servant that was sent back? And the next one after that?
5. Who did the owner finally send back? What happened to him?

Teen:
1. What did Jesus say would happen when the owner discovered what the farmers had done?
2. Match each of the following people in the parable with the person or persons that they most likely represent:

   1. the owner   a. the Jewish leaders
   2. the wicked farmers   b. Jesus
   3. the servants   c. the prophets
   4. the son   d. God

3. What do these verses say about God?

Adult:
1. Read 1 Peter 2:4, 7 and Ephesians 2:20. What is meant by Mark 12:10?
2. How did the Jewish leaders react to this parable?
3. Why were they afraid to act upon their anger?

Close in prayer thanking God that he is kind and just. Thank him for his patience with you and ask him for forgiveness for repeated sins. Ask him for strength to carry out your responsibilities in a way that is pleasing to him.

MARK 12:13-27

Discuss some of the responsibilities that we owe to our country. What responsibilities do we have to our families? How do these differ from the responsibilities we have to God?

Read Mark 12:13-27.

Child:
1. What two groups of people tried to trick Jesus (vv. 13, 18)?
2. Why were these people trying to trick Jesus (v. 13)?
3. What question did the first group ask Jesus (v. 14)?
4. How did Jesus answer their question?

Teen:
1. What question did the second group of people ask Jesus?
2. Of what did Jesus accuse them (v. 24)?
3. What does verse 25 say about life after death?

Adult:
1. How does the use of the present tense word *am* from the Old Testament quote in verse 26 prove the resurrection?
2. How do you think these two groups felt when they were through trying to trick Jesus?
3. What do these verses tell us about Jesus?

Close in prayer thanking God for your assurance as a Christian of eternal life. Thank him for his wisdom in knowing men's hearts and in dealing with us every day. Ask him for wisdom as you share your love for him and your knowledge of him with others.

MARK 12:28-34

Take turns naming some good qualities about yourself. In the following lesson, we will see why it's very important that we like ourselves, as well as others, but love God most of all.

Read Mark 12:28-34

Child:
1. Who came to Jesus and what did he ask him (v. 28)?
2. What two things did Jesus say were most important?
3. Do you love God that much?
4. What does it mean to love others as much as you love yourself?

Teen:
1. Before you can love someone else as much as you love yourself, you have to know how you feel about yourself. Would you say that you usually like yourself as you are?
2. Why does liking yourself influence the way you feel about others?
3. How do attitudes such as judging, blaming others, anger, self-righteousness, self-pity, etc. sometimes reflect our self-image?

Adult:
1. Why do you think Jesus chose these two commandments as the most important?
2. How can disobedience of these two commandments affect our relationship to God?
3. How important did the scribe say these two commandments were?
4. Is it possible to attend church regularly, read the Bible, and pray, and still not obey these two commandments?

Close in prayer thanking God for making you the person you are. Ask him to help you to love him with all your heart and to love others. Ask him to make all your actions a testimony to the fact that this love is within you.

MARK 12:35-44

Name a time when you sacrificed something (could be something material, your time, or your energy) for someone else. Why did you do this?

Read Mark 12:35-44.
Child: 1. Describe the widow and what she did (vv. 42-44).
2. Why did Jesus praise the widow?
3. How do these verses about the widow show us that how big we are or how much money we have are not important to Jesus?
Teen: 1. Name some of the things that Jesus said about the scribes in verses 38-40.
2. What do all these things tell you about the kind of people the scribes were?
3. How should the special education and opportunities of scribes cause them to act differently?
Adult: 1. Compare the act of the widow with that of the scribes and of the rich people in verse 41.
2. How do each of these groups show their belief in Jesus' teaching in verses 30 and 31.
3. In verses 35-37, Jesus proclaims that, although he is a descendant of David, he also has another relationship to David. What is it? (The Jews expected their Messiah to be from David's line. They often called Jesus "Son of David," and they thought of him as their soon-to-be political king.)

Take turns naming blessings that you have recently received. Thank God for these blessings. Ask God to help you to be willing to sacrifice your money, time, and energy for his glory.

MARK 13:1-8

Jesus, during his lifetime, always prepared his disciples for whatever they were about to experience. Discuss some things that you knew about that were going to take place (circus, elections).

In this lesson Jesus not only told what was going to take place, but also indicated what these things would mean.

Read Mark 13:1-8.

Child:
1. What did the disciples think about the temple (v. 1)?
2. Were these buildings small or large?
3. Do you think these buildings could easily be torn down?
4. What did Jesus say would happen to these buildings?

Teen:
1. What do you think the word *prophecy* means? (You may want to look this word up in the dictionary.)
2. Desire to know about the future is a human trait. Discuss some times when it would be helpful to know about the future. How could it sometimes be harmful to know the future?
3. What did Jesus say about false teachers?
4. Do you believe that Jesus prepares you to be a true follower of his, and that he will show you how to avoid following false teachers?

Adult:
1. In this passage Jesus explained about the destruction of the temple. This took place in 70 A.D. You might enjoy reading a Bible commentary to further your knowledge on this subject.

2. There are two verses in this lesson (vv. 7, 8) which tell about the last days before the second coming of Christ. Explain how you have seen some of these things taking place.
3. The protecting arm of God is always around us. Share with your family some personal experience of how God has protected you or your family.

Close in prayer thanking God for his loving watchcare over us. Thank him that, although there must come destruction and dark days, we can rejoice in the fact that he has a plan and knows the end and will always be with us. Ask him to help you to be his strong, true follower.

MARK 13:9–13

Discuss how it is much easier to face personal difficulty if you have been prepared ahead of time.

In this lesson we see how Jesus prepared his disciples for the persecution that they were to experience and how God prepares us for the life of a Christian today.

Read Mark 13:9–13.

Child:
1. Have you ever heard of any missionary or servant of God suffering for Christ's sake as Jesus predicted (v. 9)?
2. When preachers go to speak before presidents and kings they are often criticized. Tell of a modern-day preacher who has spoken in the White House.
3. How do you think the gospel can be preached to all nations (v. 10)?

Teen:
1. Do you believe that kings, presidents, governors, and other political leaders should hear the gospel? Why?
2. In this modern day we have satellites around the earth. How may these help us preach the gospel?
3. Under what circumstances could a family be divided about Christ? Remember that God told us to be obedient to our parents. How does this fit?

Adult:
1. In our doctrine of separation of Church and State, how can government officials be involved in the matter of the Kingdom of God?
2. Total dependence upon the leadership of the Holy Spirit is indicated in verse 11. Discuss what this means to each individual in times of persecution.

3. What does the word *endurance* mean to you?
4. Encourage your family to begin to think about endurance as a Christian trait. Explain the meaning of these devotions regarding their consistent, persevering, and enduring faith in Christ in these difficult days.

Close in prayer thanking God for the privelege of sharing his love with everyone. Praise him for the leadership of his Spirit in good and bad times. Ask him to keep your family together in single devotion to the Lord.

MARK 13:14-23

In times of great upheaval God prepares his children not only to survive but to understand. Describe a time of personal upheaval that you have gone through. How did God prepare you for it and at what point did you understand the purpose or necessity of it?

In this lesson Jesus tells of the destruction of Jerusalem. He gives specific instructions for that time and general instructions for all time. Quietly ask the Holy Spirit's guidance in the study of this lesson.

Read Mark 13:14-23.

Child:
1. What is a warning?
2. About what things have you been warned?
3. What warnings did Jesus give the people in these verses. (The Christians in Jerusalem listened to Jesus' warning and were saved from harm by their timely escape when the city was overtaken and destroyed.)

Teen:
1. What danger does Jesus warn about in verse 22?
2. Why do you think a person would want to imitate or pretend to be Christ or one of his prophets?
3. In what form do we sometimes see these false Christs and false prophets today?

Adult:
1. How do we see the Lord's mercy and care in verse 20?
2. Read Romans 8:18, 28. Explain the benevolent care of God even during times of tragedy.
3. Discuss the "signs" that some people become interested in today. Sometimes people get caught up in

seeing objects from outer space or other sources. Explain why we need not fear these things.

Close in prayer thanking God that we can trust his loving care and mercy. Thank him that he prepares us for times of tragedy and commit yourself into his care in total trust. Thank him that all things can be to his glory and for our good.

MARK 13:24-37

Discuss some of the things that you hope for as individuals and as a family.

One of the great promises for the Christian is the fact that Christ is coming again. Some people do not realize how clearly the Bible tells about this event. In our lesson today Jesus explains what is to take place and what our attitude toward it should be.

Read Mark 13:24-37.

Child:
1. Do you remember a day when the sun did not shine and it got very dark in the afternoon? What usually happened on that kind of day?
2. Have you ever seen a falling star?
3. What do you think about when it thunders? Does it frighten you? Why?

Teen:
1. How did Jesus describe the second coming (vv. 23-27)?
2. There are certain signs in nature that tell us of coming events. What did Jesus say about being able to determine when he was about to come again?
3. Who is the only one who knows for sure the exact date of the second coming of Christ?

Adult:
1. What command does Jesus give in verses 33, 35-37? Discuss with your family ways in which you can be prepared for Christ's return.
2. If there are children in your family, prepare them right now to be able to accept storms, earthquakes, and natural phenomena as a part of everyday life. Teach them about God's control of our daily lives.

Close in prayer praising God for the promised return of his Son. Thank him for his daily care through every difficulty. Thank him for his control over all nature as well as our lives.

MARK 14:1–11

Describe a time when you gave an expensive gift to someone. Did you enjoy saving for it, selecting it, and planning to give it? Did the person you gave it to appreciate it?

Let's see how several people treated Jesus and how he reacted to a woman who showed her love to him by giving him a very expensive gift.

Read Mark 14:1–11.

Child: 1. What were the chief priests and scribes planning to do to Jesus?
2. Describe the gift the woman brought Jesus and tell what she did with it.
3. Why were some of the people upset that she did this?

Teen: 1. Do you feel that Christians have a responsibility toward the poor? If so, how much?
2. In your opinion, was the woman in this lesson wrong to spend her money in this way? Why or why not?
3. What underlying reasons do you think some of the people had for objecting to her extravagance?
4. Why do you think Jesus appreciated the woman's gift?

Adult: 1. Discuss with your family some of your basic ideas on how you feel money should be managed.
2. In your opinion, what financial responsibilities does a Christian have toward the Lord's work?
3. Have you ever given extravagantly—beyond what you would normally give—for the cause of Christ?

4. Compare Judas with the woman in terms of their values on money.

Close in prayer thanking God for providing for your needs. Thank him too for the times when you have had more than you need. Ask him to help you to be willing to give—sometimes extravagantly—because of your love for him.

MARK 14:12-25

Discuss a time when someone you were close to moved away or took a trip and left you for awhile. How did you feel just before they left?

Have you ever had to take a trip away from your loved ones? What responsibilities did you have to take care of before you went? How did you prepare your loved ones for your absence?

Read Mark 14:12-25.

Child: 1. Have you ever helped to prepare for any kind of celebration?
2. For what special day were Jesus and his disciples getting ready (v. 12)?
3. What instructions did Jesus give his disciples?
4. What do you know about Jesus from the instructions he gave his disciples?

Teen: 1. What did Jesus know about one of his disciples?
2. Look up the word *betray* in the dictionary. In what ways do people betray others today?
3. What did some of the disciples ask about themselves? What does this tell you about them?
4. How do you account for the fact that someone who lived and walked with Jesus and knew who he was could do such a thing?

Adult: 1. What do the breaking of bread and partaking of the cup each symbolize (vv. 22-23)?
2. What is a covenant? What covenant does Jesus make at this time (vv. 24-25)?
3. Discuss the thoughts and feelings that must have been with the different ones present at the Last Supper.

4. How did Jesus prepare his disciples for the fact that he was soon going to leave them?

Close in prayer thanking Jesus for his insight into our hearts. Thank him that he cares enough for us to give us the right to decide whether or not we will stand up for him. Ask him for faithfulness to him no matter what pressures or temptations we may face.

MARK 14:26-31

Discuss the meaning of the word *loyalty*. Why is loyalty an important trait? In what situations might it be difficult to be loyal?

Read Mark 14:26-31.

Child:
1. What did Jesus predict would happen?
2. What does Peter say about this in verse 29?
3. What is Peter saying in this verse about the other disciples compared to himself?

Teen:
1. What did Jesus then predict would happen in verse 30?
2. Describe the extent of Peter's intention to be loyal to Jesus.
3. Have you ever felt that you would stand up for one of your friends regardless of who found fault with him?

Adult:
1. In what ways do adults sometimes find it hard to be loyal?
2. Why do you think Peter was so sure that he would be the one to stand by Jesus?
3. Discuss your own loyalty to Jesus. In what ways do you find it difficult in this modern society?

Close in prayer thanking Jesus for his faithfulness in caring for us and meeting our needs at all times. Ask him to help you be loyal both to him and to your friends and loved ones.

MARK 14:32-42

Discuss a time when you had a really big decision or choice to make. How did you arrive at a solution?

Read Mark 14:32-42.

Child:
1. Where did Jesus and his disciples go? Why?
2. Which disciples did Jesus take with him?
3. How did Jesus feel at this time? Why?

Teen:
1. With what decision was Jesus faced here?
2. What is the biggest decision you will ever make?
3. Discuss how decisions can sometimes affect a person for the rest of his life. Name some examples.
4. How does faith in God help in making the right decisions?

Adult:
1. How did Jesus feel when his disciples were not willing or able to stay awake during this time?
2. Why do you think the disciples were not supportive at this time?
3. How can facing a big decision or a difficult situation sometimes be a lonely time?
4. How can you best help others when they are going through a time like this?

Close in prayer thanking God for his wisdom and ability to help us to make the right decisions. Ask him to help you to always remember to turn to him when you have a decision to make and to wait for his answer.

MARK 14:43–52

Have you ever been very nice to someone's face but thought or said unkind things about him when he wasn't around?

Have you ever heard the saying "he smiles to your face while he stabs you in the back"? What does this mean? This kind of person is often called two-faced.

Judas, one of Jesus' own disciples, did something similar to this in the following lesson.

Read Mark 14:43–52.

Child:
1. Who approached Jesus in verse 43?
2. What sign did Judas and Jesus' accusers agree would be used to give Jesus away?
3. What does a kiss usually mean?
4. Why is it sad that Judas chose a kiss with which to betray Jesus?

Teen:
1. What did Judas call Jesus as he betrayed him (v. 45)? Why?
2. Who do you think was really Judas's "master" at this time?
3. What do you think caused Judas to change his allegiance? How can we be sure that this does not happen to us?

Adult:
1. How does Jesus react toward his persecutors?
2. Why do his disciples forsake Jesus at this time?
3. The young man in verses 51 and 52 is, according to some sources, supposed to be the author, Mark. What would have happened to him had he not run away.

4. Explain how fear sometimes interferes with reasoning and causes us to do things that we would not otherwise do.

Close in prayer thanking Jesus for his love for you. Thank him for his willingness to suffer loneliness and abandonment that you might know freedom from sin and eternal life. If you have never done so, ask his forgiveness for your sin and ask him to be your Savior. Ask him to forgive you for times when you have been unfaithful to him and ask him to help you to stand up for him no matter what the cost.

MARK 14:53, 55-65

Discuss the difference between the times when it is right to keep your opinions to yourself (remain silent) and when it is right to speak up and say what you think or believe about a matter.

Read Mark 14:53, 55-65.

Child:
1. Where was Jesus taken after his arrest?
2. For what purpose was he taken there?
3. What problem did Jesus' accusers face in verses 55 and 56?

Teen:
1. What was unfair about Jesus' trial?
2. Why did Jesus refuse to answer their charges (v. 60)?
3. What question was the turning point in Jesus' trial (v. 61)?

Adult:
1. To what extent did Jesus answer the high priest's question?
2. Why do you think Jesus chose to answer this particular question? What does it tell you about him?
3. What was the reaction to Jesus' statement?
4. What reason do you think these people had for reacting so violently to Jesus' claim?

Close in prayer thanking Jesus for his example of wisdom and courage. Thank him that he cared enough about you to suffer the humiliation and cruelty of these men so that you could know him as your Savior and could have forgiveness for your sins. Ask him for the courage to stand up for him whenever the opportunity arises.

MARK 14:54, 66-72

Did you ever declare that you would not succumb to a certain sin, but when the temptation actually came, you failed to resist it and did the very thing you were so sure you would never do?

Read Mark 14:54, 66-72.

Child:
1. How did Peter follow Jesus (v. 54)?
2. What does this tell you about Peter?
3. What do we already know about Peter from Mark 14:29-31?

Teen:
1. Of what did the maid accuse Peter?
2. How did Peter reply? Why?
3. Is your allegiance to Christ ever put to the test like Peter's? If so, explain how.

Adult:
1. What pressures do adults face that cause them to sometimes be reluctant to take a positive stand for Christ?
2. What did Peter feel as soon as he realized what he had done?
3. In spite of Peter's problem in this lesson, how is he perhaps braver than any of the other disciples?

Have a time of silent prayer thanking God for what he means in each of your lives. Ask him to help you to be brave and take a firm stand for him. Ask him for his forgiveness for times when fear or other selfish motives have stood in the way of your testimony for him.

MARK 15:1–15

Discuss a time when you chose to go along with the crowd rather than take a stand for what you believed to be right.

Let's see how Jesus was accused unfairly because the judge was fraid of the opinions of the crowd.

Read Mark 15:1–15.

Child:
1. In what manner was Jesus taken before Pilate (v. 1)?
2. How do you think Jesus felt when he was being brought before Pilate?
3. What custom governing prisoners did Pilate usually allow at this time of year (v. 6)?

Teen:
1. Do you think Jesus could have persuaded Pilate to release him instead of Barabbas? If so, why didn't he?
2. Why was Barabbas chosen as the one to be released rather than Jesus?
3. Why were the chief priests so anxious to put Jesus to death (v. 10)?

Adult:
1. Do you think that Pilate was convinced that Jesus was guilty?
2. Why did Pilate agree to Jesus' condemnation?
3. What might have happened to Pilate had he not gone along with the crowd?

Close in prayer thanking Jesus for the strength that he gives to take a stand for what we believe. Ask him to help you to call upon that strength. Ask him to help you remember what Jesus went through for you so that you might have the beliefs that you have.

MARK 15:16-32

Discuss how the knowledge of Jesus' death and subsequent resurrection has affected your life (for example: what changes have you made in your life, how do you look on the future, etc.).

Read Mark 15:16-32.

Child:
1. What cruel things did the soldiers do to Jesus (vv. 16-20)?
2. What was Jesus' reaction?
3. In what way did Jesus suffer this hurt for you personally?

Teen:
1. How would you feel if you were Simon and were made to carry Jesus' cross?
2. Why did Jesus refuse to take the wine that was offered him even though it might have eased some of the pain?
3. Why do you think the soldiers were interested in obtaining Jesus' garments (v. 24)?

Adult:
1. Do you think that the crowd was disappointed that Jesus refused to save himself?
2. Had he saved himself, do you think the chief priests and other religious leaders would have believed in him?
3. Why did Jesus choose not to save himself?

Discuss with your family the need for a personal acceptance and relationship with Jesus. If any member of your family does not know him, show that one how. Have a simple prayer such as the following: "Dear Lord, I realize that I have done many wrong things. I am sorry for my sins, and I ask you to forgive me. I thank you for giving your life for me, and I want you to come into my heart and live there. I want you to have control of my thoughts and actions. In Jesus's name. Amen."

If all of you have already accepted Jesus as your Savior, spend this time praying for someone you know who hasn't.

MARK 15:33-41

At the peak of his suffering Jesus, bearing the weight of our sins, felt totally separated from God.

Discuss a time when you felt alienated from God because of sin in your life.

Read Mark 15:33-41.

Child: 1. What unusual thing took place even though it was the noon hour?
2. How long did this darkness last (v. 33)?
3. Do you sometimes feel lonely at night when it's dark outside and it's time for you to go to bed?

Teen: 1. What was Jesus' cry toward the end of his suffering?
2. What do you think Jesus was feeling at this time? Why?
3. How did the crowd misunderstand his cry?

Adult: 1. Read Matthew 27:50, Luke 23:46 and John 19:30. What do these verses say about how Jesus died?
2. What was the significance of the temple curtain tearing at this time? (Read Hebrews 10:20.)
3. What did the centurion realize (v. 39)?
4. Discuss some of the other people that were present at Jesus' death. How do you think they must have felt at this time?

Close in prayer thanking Jesus for taking the weight of your sins upon himself and suffering that you might be freed from guilt and alienation from God. In a time of silent prayer, ask God's forgiveness for any known sin in your life.

MARK 15:42-47

Discuss some times when you lacked courage or self-confidence to do something that you wanted to do (for example: giving a speech, introducing yourself, witnessing to someone).

Let's see how a man acted in a confident, courageous way to do something that most people would probably be afraid to do.

Read Mark 15:42-47.

Child: 1. What day of the week was it when Jesus died (v. 42)?
2. What favor did Joseph of Arimathaea ask of Pilate?

Teen: 1. Why must it have taken courage for Joseph to ask for Jesus' body?
2. What do you think caused Joseph to have the courage to do this?
3. Why do you suppose Jesus' disciples did not offer to do this?

Adult: 1. Why was Pilate surprised that Jesus was already dead?
2. How did Joseph bury Jesus?
3. Who witnessed Jesus' burial?

Close in prayer thanking God that he gives courage when we need it if we ask him. Ask him to help you to overcome any problems that you may have in lacking the confidence or courage for each day's situations.

MARK 16:1–8

The whole Gospel of Jesus Christ hinges on the fact of his resurrection. Discuss how the Christian's assurance of eternal life because of Christ's resurrection affects your life today (for example: how does it affect your morals, activities, priorities, etc.).

Read Mark 16:1–8.

Child:
1. Why did the women come to Jesus' grave?
2. What did the women see when they got to the tomb?
3. Look up the word *resurrection* in your dictionary. What does it mean?

Teen:
1. How do you think the women felt when they discovered that Jesus' body was not in the grave?
2. Why shouldn't they have been surprised?
3. What command did the young man at the tomb give the women?
4. Why do you think he mentioned Peter specifically in his command (v. 7)?

Adult:
1. Why didn't the women obey the command that was given to them by the young man (v. 8)?
2. Discuss how you would react if you approached a loved one's grave and found the body missing.
3. How would our lives be affected had Jesus not risen from the dead?

Close in prayer thanking Jesus for his resurrection and what it means to you. Ask him to help you to be always mindful of how temporary our lives on earth are as compared with eternity. Let Christ live in your heart today.

MARK 16:9-20

Christ's death and resurrection require certain responsibilities on the part of the Christian to share his message with others.

List some ways in which you can help to carry the message of Christ's love to those who have not yet accepted Jesus as their Savior.

Read Mark 16:9-20.

Child:
1. Who was the first person to whom Jesus appeared?
2. To whom did Mary immediately go after she saw Jesus and why?
3. What were those she went to tell feeling at this time?
4. How did they react to her news?

Teen:
1. Considering the fact that Jesus had foretold his resurrection, why do you think people were so amazed and doubtful when it actually occurred?
2. How did Jesus react to the unbelief of his own disciples?
3. What commission did Jesus give his disciples (v. 15)?

Adult:
1. How does this commission apply to us today?
2. In what ways are you following his command?
3. Where did Jesus go when he finished his talk with the disciples (v. 19)?

Close in prayer thanking God for the power of his Holy Spirit in your life enabling you to follow his commission to go and tell others of his love. Ask him to make you willing and committed to obeying this command.